THE AWAKENING I COULDN'T IGNORE

DA'ZIYAH JOHNSON

Copyright © 2025 by Da'Ziyah Johnson.

All rights reserved. No part of this publication may be reproduced, distributed, or transmitted in any form or by any means, including photocopying, recording, or other electronic or mechanical methods, without the written consent of the publisher. The only exceptions are for brief quotations included in critical reviews and other noncommercial uses permitted by copyright law.

MILTON & HUGO L.L.C.
4407 Park Ave., Suite 5
Union City, NJ 07087, USA

Website: *www. miltonandhugo.com*
Hotline: *1- 888-778-0033*
Email: *info@miltonandhugo.com*

Ordering Information:
Quantity sales. Special discounts are granted to corporations, associations, and other organizations. For more information on these discounts, please reach out to the publisher using the contact information provided above.

Library of Congress Control Number: 2025917001
ISBN-13:   979-8-89285-636-2   [Paperback Edition]
            979-8-89285-637-9   [Hardback Edition]
            979-8-89285-635-5   [Digital Edition]

Rev. date: 11/04/2025

CONTENTS

Introduction vii
Chapter 1 The Mirror: Who I Thought I Was 1
Chapter 2 Roots of Pain: The Hidden
 Truths of My Childhood 5
Chapter 3 My Safety and My Scars: My Mother .. 10
Chapter 4 He Was There, But Not Really 16
Chapter 5 The struggle continues: The
 Searching for Belonging and
 Early College Years 26
Chapter 6 Faith on Shaky Grounds 34
Chapter 7 When Love Came Soft, But Cut deep . 39
Chapter 8 Trying rebuild that broken
 mirror on my own 42
Chapter 9 My breaking point and repentance 46
Chapter 10 The Realization of Truth 51
Chapter 11 The Child He Called Back 56

INTRODUCTION

One day, I recall sitting in bed and writing down everything that had been going on in my life. Authoring a book has always been my goal. I was young, stressed, and looking for a way to express myself that I could not express aloud. Then the words abruptly stopped. I had run out of things to write about.

My story was not yet complete by God.

And He still picks up the pen everyday adding a coma.

Likewise, some stories are not told because they are too painful or scared of breaking relationships that are already broken. Since no one ever inquired, mine was kept a secret.

But now I will tell you.

This is for girls like me who were supposed to remain silent, small, and motionless. Before they could even define themselves, they were labeled. This is dedicated to the daughters who do not have the parents they dreamed of the teenagers who were discarded before they could even dream, and everyone who has ever had their identity stolen before they were even aware of who they were.

This is more than just a tale.

It is a mirror.

At last, the reflection is speaking.

Chapter

1

THE MIRROR: WHO I THOUGHT I WAS

Growing up, I saw what they told me to see when I looked in the mirror.

I am a girl from a small town.

A young woman with modest aspirations.

A girl who has no real prospects.

An image that did not feel like mine was reflected by my bedroom mirror cracked on the side and stained with age. For a place that did not believe much outside of its boundaries, I saw a girl who walked a little too proudly and laughed a little too loudly.

The girl did not have a father until she was eight years old. Which felt more like a guest star than a permanent role. Girls like me were expected to become pregnant as soon as they reached their teenage years, right? All because "teenage pregnancy was real," If they got to know me and believed in me. Teenage pregnancy did not exist in my head.

The thing they never grasped, though, is that I had big dreams.

I did not say it aloud because it was risky to dream aloud in a place like mine. It turned you into a target. It sparked a conversation. Talking is also a sport in small towns. Forgiveness moves more slowly than judgment, and gossip moves more quickly than grace. I discovered that early. You are everything they told their daughters not to be after just one inappropriate outfit, one late night, or one honest moment.

Everyone knew your grandma and remembered your mama's business, even when she tried to bury it, and I grew up in a place where dreams were as close together as church pews. A place where the streets and walls both had eyes and ears, and neither was nice. Right when you think you were waiting until everyone went to bed to do things. It did not matter what happened in the town, what was said at what time, it was closed, and the lights were out before 8pm. Whatever happened during quiet time everybody knew first thing before the sun even rose.

Opportunities came and went without knocking. And hardly anyone who stayed looked up. They used survival as a metric and even had guidelines. Instead of being lost, opportunities were never presented. They were too

THE AWAKENING I COULDN'T IGNORE

quiet for anyone to notice, moving past the front door like shadows. We were taught to prepare for impact rather than to pursue our dreams. to survive until the following day without collapsing.

Growth and healing were not discussed by those in my immediate vicinity. They used the ability to keep your head down without breaking like a yardstick for life. Survival was a set of rules, not just a way of being. Keep quiet. Avoid complaining. Keep your emotions in check. Do not keep elevated expectations. You were weak if you wept. You were disrespectful if you spoke up. You were unappreciative if you desired more.

We were shaped more by unspoken expectations than by clear guidance:

Do not respond.

Limit the number of questions you ask.

Do not believe that you are better than other people.

And do not think you're going anywhere.

They made it seem like my failure was an unstoppable force.

What is worse?

They nearly succeeded.

There were times such as when I found out that someone had taken out $74,000 in student loans in my name. The location that it went back to was mind blowing. 13. Before I stepped on a college campus or applied. Prior to my knowledge of interest rates.

Someone had already made up their mind about who I would not become. They saw my defeat before my match could even start.

However, there is a risk associated with a girl who begins to wake up. About a girl who begins to inquire, who begins to see herself in a way that goes beyond what the town whispers and what the mirror reflects.

Through God she will never close her eyes again.

Chapter

2

ROOTS OF PAIN: THE HIDDEN TRUTHS OF MY CHILDHOOD

I cannot tell you much about our financial struggles as a child because my mother made sure I did not experience them. I was not hungry when I went to bed. I was wearing shoes. And for some reason, she never let it show on her face, even if the lights flickered or the rent was not paid. I did not know if it was ever a time if it truly happened.

However, that does not mean I did not struggle, even if we did not struggle visible.

I had mental difficulties.

I had emotional difficulties.

I also had physical difficulties.

It was not always growing up without anything that caused pain. Pain appeared silently at times. Occasionally in shaken tones over minor issues that grew into more significant ones. Occasionally, it manifested as the piercing pain of having my name called just for being there. Or making too much noise. Or too honest. Or simply too much.

I was constantly on the move, bouncing from one house to another like a suitcase that no one wanted to carry around for extraordinarily long. I never knew or asked why I just knew my mom was young, and she was doing the best she can. I just wish she were softer spoken than the hardness she showed on me because of her problems.

My aunt shared her home with my mom and me. My great-aunt. My grandmother. I once lived in trailer parks and apartments that were considered "projects." Then it went back to my grandmother's house. We eventually moved into our own home, but by then, I was already experiencing a sense of chaos. Early on, I realized that home was not always a physical location but rather a person who provided security.

For me, from what I can remember those individuals were my mom's mother, my grandmother, my Godmother, and older cousins.

My favorite one was my mom's mother.

I recall the scent of the magic blue hair grease she used to comb my hair, the softness of her nightgown, and the sensation of crawling into her bed. Her voice would hum something old and familiar as I sat between her knees and watched her fix my hair. She would first grease my scalp before greasing my forehead like that is a part of my hair. And those mornings were enough to give me a sense of completeness for a while.

However, she also carried her own sorrows and regrets. I was unaware at the time, but life had dragged her in unexpected directions. Although she could not provide the kind of support she desired for her children, she did her best for her grandchildren. Always.

She had a stroke, which woke her up like a robber in the night. Nobody but God did that. I noticed how she changed, slowed down, and spoke in a unique way. For the first time, I realized she was not stoppable even though her strength declined in front of me. Something in me was shaken by that.

Prior to that and after, though, she was my source of stability in an unstable world. Along with my aunts and older cousins.

Regarding my mother, we experienced both love and conflict. I will not lie I had a mouth on me. However, I was truthful. I always spoke the truth, even if it made others uncomfortable. It was the delivery, not the truth itself, that I had to get used to.

I occasionally received whooping for my actions.

I occasionally received them for things I didn't do.

I also occasionally got them for no other reason.

What I experienced was not the most difficult aspect of growing up. The reason for this was that nobody really questioned why I was the way I was. They did not see the pain, but they did see the attitude. They did not see the defense, but they did see the opposition. They could see the isolation, but not the noise.

More times than I can recall, I went to school wearing wet clothes. I didn't want to. However, I still had to leave because my mother would forget to put my clothes in the dryer and was rushing to get me to school for whatever reason. Most of the time, I would sit there not knowing what was going on, but I knew my clothes were wet. I was only 3 or 4.

However, my Head Start teachers took notice. They would call my aunt rather than my mother if I did not have clothes already there. Request that she bring some dry clothes. Or get me to change and come back. That gave me more information than I was prepared to receive.

For me, childhood was a sequence of silent awakenings. I had realizations that I was unaware of until much later. For example, I did not know my father's identity until I was eight years old. Not because I investigated it. However, it was time to finally meet the man who had helped create me but not raise me. That was the beginning of how God had planned my rescue and make my big dreams unfold right before my eyes.

Not knowing where half of you originate from is painful. And a deeper one in knowing at last and questioning whether it was better not to.

However, I will say this:

Sometimes I had no idea what was broken around me.

However, I sensed it.

I was also learning how to keep myself together.

Because I was certain that despite all the chaos, the soaked clothes, the missed birthdays, and the bouncing houses, there was something inside of me that would not give up. There was a whisper that you were meant for more. God kept knocking and making his presences known.

I simply have not come to terms with it yet.

Chapter

3

MY SAFETY AND MY SCARS: MY MOTHER

I adore my mother; I do not always agree with her.

Isn't that the difficult part?

When the person you love the most causes you the greatest pain.

When the location that should feel the safest turns into your first battleground.

Her womb was not the only thing that shaped me. Her words shaped who I am. Her palms. Her responses. Her quiet. And at times her absence.

More times than I can remember, she called me by name. Sometimes it was out of frustration, sometimes out of rage, and sometimes just because. Lessons were not always learned from whooping. They arrived quickly, unexpectedly, and frequently without cause.

THE AWAKENING I COULDN'T IGNORE

I can still clearly remember that Sunday at church.

During service, my younger brother was making noise and making hits on me. I was gently nudging, whispering, and begging him to stop. Then she struck me, though. Suddenly. I impulsively swung my arm back, thinking it was him, only to discover too late that it was her. And I froze when I realized it.

I knew I was taught to always obey your parents or if you do not, your days will be shortened.

I felt shame more quickly than the slap. I did not hold out for the others.

I knew how my mother was already, so I went outside of that church. She came behind me yelling and we went home.

She did exactly what I expected her to do, which was tell everyone after church service who saw it and called to be nosy that I had hit her. She claimed that I was rude and made sure her version of the story was seen by everyone.

After that, they wanted to speak with me. My Head Start teacher to be exact. My mom took me to her house and said my childhood friend wanted to play with me, but it was asking me to elaborate. Why was I being disrespectful? I was truly shocked because that is not what had happened. I explained to her what truly happened, and once my mom came to pick me up, I said nothing. I held that in I knew if I tried to speak up, she was going to say I was being rude and give me a whooping like I was someone on the street.

Through God, my aunt was my only savior that day. She defended me after seeing the entire incident. Even though my mother did not want to hear it, I told her the truth. She was familiar with me. She was aware that I would never intentionally hit my mother. However, it did not matter at the time because my mother disliked the truth that contradicted her story.

And I spent most of my childhood that way.

My mother was a reckless person who acted without thinking and blamed her past for every explosion. She claimed to have experienced trauma. She did. But I did too. And unlike her, I did not use it to harm others. I did not make it a problem for anybody else.

She struck me in the head with a glass jar one day.

About something so small. I did not deserve that. I recall the pain. The blood.

That was the tipping point for me.

With my head still bleeding, I sprinted to my grandmother's house with my cousins and picked up the phone. I called my father. "I'm ready to move," I said to him.

It was on Friday when I called.

THE AWAKENING I COULDN'T IGNORE

I was on a plane on Tuesday.

I always said I was grateful for my dad for that, but I never gave God credit for that when it was the help of him who led my dad to react so fast.

Once I was sent to New York; My mom informed everyone, "for better opportunities."

The fact is, though, I made the decision to leave.

I went with survival.

My parents frequently did that: They took credit for the good but never took responsibility for the bad.

However, the trauma always had my number, regardless of how far I moved.

What I believed would be my relief, my new beginning...

It was just a change from one type of trauma to another.

I saw her endure actual, horrifying abuse at the hands of men. I recall my younger brother being afraid, and me not being there to keep him safe. I was the oldest. I should have been present, but God was. I was not there because I had recently moved out to live with my father. I lived with that guilt of wishing we had the same dad.

The flames from the fire that destroyed her house are still visible to me.

When it happened, my younger brother was with her.

The guy who did it? Walked off after giving him a wrist slap.

Since his cousin was the police who showed up.

The world we lived in was like that. That should also explain how small the town we live in is.

Trauma found a way to follow me just when I was far enough away to keep my peace.

Imagine waking up believing it was finally over.

You pick up your phone and launch Snapchat, where you see videos and status updates about a dozen police officers around your mother's apartment building.

I did not give it much thought at first. It could be the neighbors or something random.

Then I received the call, though.

My brother was the one.

His voice wavered when he opened his mouth.

Once more, I am afraid. He did not even want to go back to the apartment.

The same man who once destroyed her home with fire.

The same individual. Once more, back. Putting his hands on her again in front of my brother this time.

Furthermore, I was not present.

I was absent once more.

I left to be free, but since I still had to observe the cycle, freedom did not feel like peace. I was baffled: When would she figure it out? When was the pattern going to break?

You would really think it got better after this, but it didn't. I grew up apologizing for existing.

Chapter

4

HE WAS THERE, BUT NOT REALLY

He had already established a life without me before we ever met.

My mother claims that he had recently got married and had what they believed to be his first child when she told him about me. However, I was his oldest child. According to my mother, she only wanted him in my life and did not want him for herself. I have always remembered that part. She could have resented or fought. However, "Be there," she said simply.

My grandmother, his mother, came to greet me first. When she first saw me, I can still clearly recall her saying, "No DNA test needed," without hesitation. That is his child. Nevertheless, we conducted the test, and the findings supported what everyone had already observed. I was his child. I was the boy version of him, they said. The same eyes. same nose. The same goes for everything.

I took my first flight a month later. I flew with his mom, who I now call granny, to meet him when I was eight years old.

I felt unprepared when I got there. I didn't really know him. My grandmother, who had already accepted me without question, provided me with more comfort than he did. I was afraid of how to ask and even more afraid of what to call him when I asked if I could go stay with her. However, I asked. "No," he replied.

Sad and practically pleading without words, I turned to her. "No," he said.

All I wanted to do in my mind was return home. I permitted myself by saying that my mom had just given birth to my younger brother the previous month. I did not know how to say that aloud, and I was not prepared.

But something changed. Slowly.

I started to have a good relationship with him.

I loved him, and he loved me.

I can still clearly recall one of my first genuine encounters with my uncle, who is also his brother. He inquired about my musical preferences. I said, "Gospel," without even thinking about it.

He gave me a look that was simultaneously shocked, delighted, and proud. He was not expecting that response from someone so young, I could tell.

My favorite song at the time was Tamela Mann's "Take Me to the King." Presumably expecting me to hum a few lines, he played it for me. He was stunned, however, when I sang it all, word for word, with all my little heart. His face showed me. He was taken aback. He was proud, though.
Even though I did not fully comprehend it at the time, I used to cry every time I heard songs like that one by myself. I just knew that tears were falling, but I had no idea why. I now realize that it was a deeper, more spiritual thing. God was stirring something inside of me even then. I was drawn even then.

Not because of the song, but because I felt seen at last, that moment with my uncle remained with me. It was one of the first times I had the impression that someone had seen something profound within me, even though I had not fully realized it myself.

Weeks later it was time for me to go home to Alabama, I only visited New York twice a year after that. He would always ask, "Would you like to live with me?" And each time, I will try to think more deeply. Until I finally said yes at the age of 13.

Everything was new when I moved in: the house, the rules, and the state. I recall doing things I had never done before when I went to church with them. That is when it happened.

My first deep spiritual awakening.

God's presence was so clear to me. I sensed that He was guiding me rather than punishing me. And I believed even though I did not understand every step of walking with Him. I gave my life to him when I was thirteen years old. What surrender meant was unknown to me. I had no idea what discipleship was. However, I had faith.

Not long afterward, I learned something that made me cry: my Godmother had been praying for me ever since I was conceived. For years, she had prayed to God that I would one day surrender my life to Him, become the leader He had intended me to be, and make a difference in the world.

I was able to weather storms I never anticipated because of that same quiet faith that my Godmother had sown.

Because it turned out to be something different from what I had anticipated, a new life, a healing one. In the end, I returned to Alabama shortly after. One academic year. That was all that was required.

My dad and his wife had a difficult year. I felt like I was a burden to them.

There were restrictions on their definition of love. The rules that came with their parenting style were not always fair. The Holy Spirit then began to persuade me once more. So, I paid attention. I went back to New York. I had an inner voice telling me to be strong. Wait a moment. There is more to come.

I listened to that voice when I was 15. I was still unaware that it was God. However, I do now.

I recalled the occasions when they had purchased items for me, but they would later return them due to my demeanor, or more accurately, my tone. My mother would always be the fallback option. She would feel compelled to get me whatever they took back when I returned home feeling depressed or angry. It resembled an undercover parental competition.

The most painful thing, though, was witnessing their different treatment of my younger sister. When I first moved in, she was 5 years old. She has an attitude that beat mines, and she is the same age as I was then. She has never had anything taken away from her like I did. My stuff was sent back to the store. They do not threaten to discipline her for her tone the way I was. She is not labeled the way they labeled me.

Without my mother's consent, they started me on birth control when I was thirteen.

I first heard the statement, "Teenage pregnancy is real," at that point. As if my future had already been predetermined. However, that was not even on my mind. Not at thirteen.

And now? Although I love my sister.

My sister is thirteen years old. No birth control. No suspicion. Not a threat. No labels. Simply love.

I was aware that the birth control had a negative effect on me. I wanted to leave. I told my doctor the truth during a check-up when no one else was present. I did not engage in sexual activity. I did not make this choice. I wanted to leave. After giving me a quick glance and a gentle nod, she said, "All right. We will keep it a secret. Additionally, remember me whenever you write your book or film."

Here it is, then. You mentioned it. Thank you.

However, my stepmother discovered that I had not received the vaccination.

She also involved my dad.

"Either get the shot or go back to Alabama," they said as they seated me.

What parent would send their child back to the place that caused them to break? I sobbed.

However, I stayed up.

Since I was aware that I could not turn back. I went to get that shot.

They believed they were keeping me safe. However, it did not feel like a shield. It was a sense of control. As if I were always being watched. As if I was only loved when I did what they said.

I broke it again as a result. Silently. Not entirely, though.

Because God was still there and he saw everything.

"Hold on," he whispered repeatedly. I remain here.

And even though my father was the last person to influence my suffering, God still made use of it.

To fulfill my mission.

To awaken me.

I realized then that there were layers to survival. Running was not the only thing involved. At times, it was about perseverance.

I always knew that I would never return to staying after I graduated. I will move away to attend college. When the time came, I barely survived the visits.

I held on to the fact that I was already on track to graduate a full year earlier. During my stay, I hardly left my room. Everything I did or said seemed to be used against me. I would intentionally write things and leave them out in the hopes that they would read them and relate to how I felt, but instead they would wake me mad and ask me why I had written them. All I wanted was to express myself without getting shouted at or labeled impolite. However, I was unable to.

Social media became my outlet, and I eventually began posting online. It was spiteful at times. How much they were hurting me was something I wanted them to see. However, as time went on, I discovered through God that once someone slaps you on the cheek turn and give them your other cheek to slap.

Mostly due to my mouth, I recall getting into trouble. I am always honest. I simply could not control it. My birthday then arrived.

It was the worst. Before they went all out for my birthday, I always got what I asked for but this time around things had taken a turn. I had the best birthday when covid-19 was around then when it was time for this last one, my last birthday spent with them. I took everything in knowing I would never turn back unless I visited.

Not a cake. No celebration. Just two gifts and permission to hang out with my friends. That was it. They all went out with balloons, decorations, and everything else for my youngest sister's birthday, which was a few months later. I paid no mind but somehow my middle sister did. "They're going all out for her birthday, but they did not do this for yours," my middle sister said aloud. I chuckled. since she was correct. I went on and repeated what she said.

I did experience some sort of emotion. However, I kept it to myself. I simply gave my sister time. She was younger than me, so of course I was not jealous.

I just accepted I was an outside child and on rare occasions I received the same treatment as an outside child would.

Then the last blow was delivered.

Because her daughter told her what was said, my stepmother's mother, someone I absolutely loved, became enraged, and called me by name. My real grandparents never did that before so of course I was heated. Four months before graduation, we got into an argument, and I was kicked out of the house as a result. Of course, they said I picked to move out to make them look good, but that was not the case. I was verbally told to get out "I don't want her here" and my dad allowed it.

He didn't mind it at all. I always hoped one day he would defend me, but he never did.

Knowing that I was going to graduate a full year early and that returning would practically ensure I could not, they were fine with sending me back to Alabama.

However, God had a different idea.

My dad's mother, my grandmother, would not have it. Like she always did, she defended me. I stayed at her house until I graduated.

When my stepmother arrived, she threw all my belongings in black trash bags on her front porch.

Still, I surpassed the odds.

I received my diploma. A year ahead of schedule.

I forgave them despite everything. I also expressed regret for my mistakes. I tried to proceed.

However, they were still focused on my former self.

Time went by. And my dad stopped communicating with me once more.

He only gives me a call on Christmas or my birthday. That is all.

And the memory of the first eight years without him is brought back, along with the pain. It is bittersweet to see my sisters get the father I've always desired. Although it hurts me, it is a blessing for them.

Because I secretly want my father.

Chapter

5

THE STRUGGLE CONTINUES: THE SEARCHING FOR BELONGING AND EARLY COLLEGE YEARS

After high school, I returned to Alabama to await the start of my first year of college. Going back was something I had always dreaded, and as I grew older, I became more aware of how much I detested it.

I had pride in half the city, but what about the other half? Crazy. Resentful.

There were rumors that some of the girls wanted to fight with me. I was superior to everyone else, they said. In fact, they were unaware of what I had gone through in New York. I concealed the shattered fragments behind my smile. They only saw the joyful side of me.

THE AWAKENING I COULDN'T IGNORE

The murmurs eventually escalated into conflict. They called me scared when one of the girls approached me, despite my repeated assurances that I did not want to fight. That was enough to make me feel something. I did not back down from anything in middle school, as everyone knew. So, I gave in and fought with her.

I heard a voice on the way to the fight.

"You are not this person. Do not allow narrow-minded people to hold you back as you prepare to enter college."

I did not listen, though. And I lost that battle at the end of the fight. Something more profound than a mere physical altercation. I was no longer the person I was becoming.

I decided which school I would attend that same week. I picked the unexpected HBCU out of the 55 that accepted me. I never had time to carefully consider my options during my senior year because I was so preoccupied. Furthermore, it did not seem like anyone cared if I attended college after I was kicked out of my dad's house.

For someone else, someone I thought of as family, they threw a farewell party, but not for me. Unlike other times, my stepmother never inquired about my whereabouts or how they could assist. Neither did my father. They had abandoned me already.

However, God had not.

Despite my fear, I was determined to start school. Despite knowing no one, I was determined to succeed. Since I was a young child, I had been classified as someone who would not go extremely far. I was prepared to disprove them.

I had a good relationship with my roommate right away. It was the four of us until she transferred, at which point it was just the three of us. She discovered that some of the girls she had gone to middle school with were in our hallway. Even now, we remain together.

I arrived determined to still have good grades. I had no intention of playing around with my education.

However, it was meant to be a new beginning at college. A location where I could at last embrace my true self. Instead, it turned into another battleground where I was struggling in silence with pain, identity, and purpose while attempting to maintain a positive attitude as if nothing was wrong.

Even though there were people all around me, I still felt totally alone. I was slowly getting over my past wounds. On some days, it felt more like hiding than healing.

I was still looking for love and boys. As if someone had already authored my story for me, I was introduced to sex too early and started taking birth control at the age of thirteen without my mother's consent.

THE AWAKENING I COULDN'T IGNORE

I tried it at the age of sixteen. Furthermore, I was unable to distinguish between lust and love by the time I started college. I assumed it was typical. It seemed fine to me.

During my first year, I did not go out much. We had a midnight curfew, and I was usually in bed not because I was flawless, but because I understood what I was losing.

I did not meet my academic advisor, who would end up being like a second father to me, until the end of that year. He inquired about my background, my early years, and my identity outside of my grades before we even started organizing my schedule for the spring semester of my first year.

I was not accustomed to it. But it really got to me. It dawned on me then that there was a reason God had put him in my life. I genuinely do not know where I would be without him.

Everything felt different when I returned home for the first time since I started college. The silent resentment was palpable to me. Nobody anticipated that I would make it this far. Some even inquired, "Are you still enrolled in school?"

Indeed. I continue to attend school.

When I returned to campus after our first break ended during my first year, I was enrolled in several classes taught by my advisor.

Naturally, God never failed to remind me that He was still present in my life. I recall having to give a presentation in one of my advisor's classes. To demonstrate that we were attending and that we were taking something tangible with us when we left, we were required to give a presentation on a lesson he had taught. I was afraid because the class was full of upper-class students. I was at a loss as to what to say. I started out in a group before deciding to go alone.

I switched topics at least half a dozen times. "God, I don't know what I'm doing," I finally sobbed.

It was not until now that I realized He was listening.

That is when I had the idea. I related the Bible to globalization. I had not been listening, but my advisor had already been explaining to us how globalization relates to scripture and current events. I began to see that it was intentional.

I talked about how we should be fruitful, multiply, and replenish. Knowing what is right but still choosing to do wrong is a sin, I explained to the class. I expressed my opinion that the racial wealth gap may have been caused by those who recognize the benefits of globalization but do not adequately educate others about it.

I had no idea that the Holy Spirit was speaking through me while I was giving my presentation. I continued by quoting the Bible's instruction to "be fruitful and increase in number and fill the earth." I asked the class to consider how the scripture might apply to our resources, even though it was originally discussing something else. What if we increased our wealth and knowledge and then reinvested it in our communities?

Change is constantly demanded, but no one wants to be a part of it. I begged God for breakthrough, clarity, and peace for years, demanding change. I kept wondering why my life never seemed to change. Why do I continue to feel stuck? However, the reality is I was not working as hard as God had commanded. I was acting according to my own terms, not his.

I was still receiving messages from the Holy Spirit. I had just not yet noticed it. That was one of the messages that clearly went over my head.

The same way my Godmother prayer went over my head.

In my heart, I wanted to change, but I was not sure where to begin. I aspired to develop into a person who could help others and who carried light rather than just scars. I was still heading in the wrong direction, but my heart was calling for more.

Sophomore year, I stayed focused on grades, on growing, on healing. I started forgiving people I never thought I would forgive. I was learning more about who I was. But I also started going out to more parties and events and sometimes, I lost control.

I was overly drunk one evening. Someone took advantage of me without my consent. I vowed never to drink in front of boys ever again. Then again, I was sober, and it happened. "No," I replied. He was indifferent. In any case, he got what he wanted.

In silence, I sobbed as I lay there. I had no one to contact me. Not even my dad. He only gives me calls on my birthday and Christmas. So why would I feel comfortable calling him to cry?

However, my friend allowed me to cry in her arms the moment I got back to my room.

I thought I would be protected if I had a boyfriend. However, each guy who followed only made me feel worse. I came to the realization that God did not want me to have sex. He did not want me to consume alcohol. He did not want me to go out. And with all that trauma, he most certainly did not want me to settle for who I was.

I was not listening, though.

I gave in to lust.

Because I had never learned the difference from anyone.

They told me that teen pregnancy is real when I was thirteen, but they never mentioned that God's love is even more real.

But once more, I was accumulating old trauma on top of new trauma without really knowing it and having no way to let it out. Helping others, keeping busy, and doing everything I could to keep everything together, I kept adding more to my plate.

Because I was depending on my own strength rather than God's, I was unaware of how exhausted I was.

Chapter

6

FAITH ON SHAKY GROUNDS

As my sophomore year ended, I noticed I was avoiding it more and more. It was too much for me to handle. In addition to serving as the Junior Class Vice President and Head Residential Advisor for my dorm, I also held a few other leadership roles that, while admirable on paper, were gradually consuming me. I was diverting my attention, but I convinced myself that I was being productive and developing into the woman I was destined to be. I was sprinting.

I was aware of God at that time, but not really. I said some prayers, but they seemed pointless. I read my Bible, but I did not understand a word. I was still too much of a part of the outside world. I remained spiritually numb because I was still too attached to people, routines, and circumstances.

I discovered the hard way the enemy did not care how much I prayed or how many scriptures I read if he knew he had control over me. Furthermore, God was not happy either. He did not desire fragments of me. He desired me in my own way.

I instead poured myself into other people. To everyone who needed something, I said "yes." I tried to be strong for everyone but myself. And it was not until I was completely exhausted that I realized how exhausted I was.

My advisor/father figure noticed it. I spent more time in his office trying to recharge for a moment. Whether he realized it or not, his words, encouragement, and love for all of us students kept me going.

His office turned into a peaceful place for me. a secure location.

Suddenly, it was time to create my junior year schedule. One more semester. Another journey back to a place that had lost its sense of home. I kept thinking that things would be different this time. Perhaps returning would not hurt as much as I could. However, I was mistaken.

The only reason it felt better the last time was because people were shocked to see how far I had gone. I should not have made it this far. Not in line with their account. I was still standing, though.
And I didn't have a thought about giving up at the time.

I was still exhausted. My faith was in jeopardy. Despite my good intentions, I was acting in the wrong way. I had no idea that I was constructing my life on a shaky foundation. I was not operating out of surrender, but rather out of habit, hustle, and trauma.

And the consequences of that would soon be overwhelming.

But everything fell apart again right when I felt like I was finally moving on from some past pain and in a good place.

With what I believed to be a genuine and healing heart, I had reached out to my stepmother. I apologized, acknowledged my mistakes, and expressed my forgiveness to her for the ways she had wronged me. I did it because I genuinely wanted peace, even though it was not easy. We were beginning anew. God was fixing something that had been damaged.

However, I discovered a month later that she had been discussing behind my back. Revealing I had "mental health" problems with others. after everything. after I approached her with humility and love. I was devastated by that.

Since I had been there, I had asked my dad if he thought I was acting out or doing something improper. "No," he said. "Everything seems fine," he said.

THE AWAKENING I COULDN'T IGNORE

However, everything changed the moment I explained my request to him, and she intervened. Suddenly, I was the issue again. All my words and emotions suddenly became meaningless. And I cannot describe how much that hurt.

I was venting to my best friend while having my hair done. I was completely unaware of the stylist's close relationship with my stepmother. I was just speaking—truthfully. stating that my father had never been as present for me as he had been for my younger sisters. Even though I believed that we had moved on to a better place, I had always felt that my stepmother did not like me. I was attempting to make sense of everything and determine what I had done to deserve her treatment in the first place.

However, her friend allowed her to overhear the entire conversation. I had no idea. Simply put, that was a violation. That is her friend, indeed. However, that did not make it correct.

This is what happened when I mentioned the mental health comment with my dad because it hurtful. profoundly. Even though I am still figuring things out on my own, I have been working hard to get better, show up more, and heal.

She suddenly turned something I had confided in into a weapon. Yes, I did once say that I wanted to see a counselor, but especially in families like mine, people like to dismiss the term "mental health" as if it were a joke. And that is unacceptable.

She flipped the script and used what I said during that phone call as a diversion rather than taking responsibility for what she said about me. She ducked. To avoid taking responsibility for her initial backstabbing, she made me the antagonist.

I was simply sick of keeping everything to myself; I was not attempting to attack anyone. But he misinterpreted it. I was not heard by him.

Yes, I had a father in terms of money. But on an emotional level? mentality? Physically, even? He was not present.

I was reminded once more that I had been attempting to hold everything together on my own strength rather than God's, trying to construct healing on top of unresolved trauma. And I was exhausted.

Chapter

7

WHEN LOVE CAME SOFT, BUT CUT DEEP

During all that suffering, I met him.

I was still getting over the boys who had come before him, boys who had already left their scars—in my sophomore year. I convinced myself that I was prepared for something genuine. that perhaps things would be different this time.

I was still broken, though. Still looking. Spiritually numb as ever. I was not even aware that the spirit of lust had already encircled me. Though I was only attending to a deeper need, I mistakenly believed that I was choosing love. The kind of need that attention pretends to satisfy but never really does.

It was light, enjoyable, and simple at first. Then came talks about "us," continuous communication, and late-night chats. regarding the future. Regarding the meaning of being together.

And everything changed right when I believed I could trust it.

I discovered that I was alone. Other girls were present. several. He claimed he was lying to protect me when I confronted him. Calling a lie protection—imagine that.

I was completely unaware of it. Since I knew where he was, I didn't question anything. Location, however, does not equate to loyalty. He claimed to be evolving. that his goal was to perform better. However, he kept changing his words:

"I'm changing."

"I want us to be together."

"I am not prepared to be in a relationship."

"Let's be friends."

Heartfelt messages

Again, and again.

I was aware that it was unhealthy. But I couldn't let go of my heart. And honestly? A piece of mine hasn't yet. Not in a crisis. Not how it was. However, in a silent pain that I will never forget.

I just pray for him now. from afar. I pray that God will enable him to develop into the man I once glimpsed.

Not for me, perhaps. Not for me, perhaps. But for a person who really deserves it.

I still adore him. I'm still concerned. However, he caused me too much pain. And I can't ignore that any longer.

That's it, That's all.

Chapter

8

TRYING REBUILD THAT BROKEN MIRROR ON MY OWN

Things started changing in my junior year. Silently. Gently. However, I sensed it.

I stopped visiting my advisor's office for the free recharge sessions he had always provided. He saw. He did, of course. Even though my grades remained stable, I stopped attending classes as frequently as I once did. He saw through that, though. He did.

I would bow my head whenever I saw him on campus outside of class. I was unwilling to speak. I was aware that he would say something. And he did. Each time.

What could I say, though? I was still struggling. I am still battling lust. I am still confused about believing I was in love with someone who was not truly mine. who was not truly intended for me. Trying to make broken things feel whole had worn my heart out.

I remained extremely busy. I attended all events, meetings, and activities. particularly in the capacity of Head Residential Advisor. I was essential to my team. My residents held me in high regard. I served as their haven away from home, their listening ear, and their haven. I smiled as I bore the suffering of everyone else. As if I had none of my own.

However, I did.

And then everything fell apart.

I began letting go of the things that used to divert me, one by one, first the drinking, then the parties. At first, I did not even understand why. I simply knew that I had lost interest. When my friends pleaded with me to go out, I would politely decline. They thought that was crazy, especially since I used to be the one who was constantly trying to get somewhere. Despite being the youngest, they used to refer to me as the group's mother. Now, though, I am the mother. the assigned driver. The accountable one. The person who waited all night to ensure that everyone returned safely was a safe place.

But what is behind all of that? I was having trouble.

I lay in bed in silence for days. numb. Not moving. I was unsure of the issue. I was unable to identify it. All I felt was emptiness.

Then the last straw appeared.

I deliberately chose not to sit for a final exam. It was on the internet. I just needed to sign in. However, I lacked strength. I realized then that something was seriously amiss.

The girl who had been on the Dean's List each semester since college began, who had excelled academically since kindergarten, had just failed a class. Intentionally.

"Here I am, God," I recall saying. What is the matter with me?

I then resumed attending church. I grabbed my Bible. attempted to interpret the confusion.

I grew more convinced the more I looked for Him. It felt heavier the deeper I went. Inside of me, the things I believed I had dealt with were still alive. I prayed louder. My nights grew longer. My heart was raw.

However, I was looking.

And that had some significance.

I even made the decision to get baptized because I felt like I was finally acting morally. One day, I told my advisor about it and that the date was approaching February.

He simply gazed at me. "February?"

I paused at the way he said it. He then calmly and gently started to explain a few things about Christ and church. He did not advise me against it. He did not dispute. But in hindsight, he was suppressing something through the holy spirit that clearly once again went over my head.

"When you're ready to ask me questions, ask them, I'm here" he said.

I heard him.

However, I did not understand him.

Not until the last minute.

Looking back, I wish I had done more research, as I do now. I might have avoided having a headache. However, I am also aware that everything occurs for a reason.

Particularly when attempting to fix a damaged mirror by yourself. All the fissures and reflections reveal things you tried to ignore.

And just when I was reassembling the pieces...

Once more, I broke it.

Chapter

9

MY BREAKING POINT AND REPENTANCE

When the time came, I was "baptized," but not in a setting that genuinely gave God the respect He so richly deserved. And did He take that lightly, in your opinion? Considering how many times I turned away from him when he tried to reach me? Oh, no. He would not let me sleep until I fixed it.

I was getting better reading my Bible more and occasionally praying. However, it was not hitting as hard as it is now. I assumed the enemy was upset because I was evolving, but he was giggling. He was laughing because, like him, I was abusing everything that God had taught me while feigning to know Him.

I realized then that I needed to start putting things right, especially with my stepmother. I sent her a message expressing my forgiveness. Since she made that critical remark about mental health, we had not communicated, and she never got back to me. However, that was all right. I did it to set her and myself free, not to get a response. Before you leave, God says, try to make peace. So, I did. And I am grateful that He revealed the truth to me about everything.

Then the defeats arrived. One friend after another began to fade. Problem after problem. "God, please—I can't take this," I screamed. Except for the one person I thought I would lose at first, it seemed like everyone had left.

I continued to share everything with my advisor. I had to. Life was too harsh.

I eventually resigned from my position as Head RA. I had to stop playing the part. While I was breaking inside, I was arguing with my boss, my team, and students. I was no longer that person. I began acting in ways that were completely out of character for me. And nobody appeared to comprehend. There was nothing left for me to argue with, and everyone had something to say.

Yes, I was changing, but I was still attempting to manage everything without God's help. At that point, everything fell apart.

People started to turn against me. Show me no respect. They were looking for an excuse to despise me. To be honest, I gave up trying to resist it. Then God reminded me, "I look low, I sit high." Everything is visible to me. I am aware of reality. And I understood how could

He stand up for me while I continued to turn my back on Him?

Everything struck me at once one night: my dad, my stepmother, my childhood pain, the stress of being a RA, and loneliness. I attempted suicide.

I was merely the battlefield in what felt like a spiritual tug-of-war, with God on one side and the devil on the other.

"Stop," I heard God say. Put it down. I did not hear.

"All right," he said. I will come to your rescue. But in the process, I will impart a lesson to you.

People inquire as to how I was able to call for assistance. I called myself. Because I knew deep down that I would go to hell if I died that night. Furthermore, I deserved to be called home by the same God who created me. Not me. The devil, no.

The ambulance arrived. Once I got to the hospital, I felt like everything was gone. They dressed me like a suicide watch. As I saw one doctor after another, they all asked the same questions, and I realized I was sane. I was not myself just for a moment.

Nevertheless, I had to visit a mental health facility. Although I've never been to jail it had the feel of jail. I had to stay until Tuesday after arriving on Friday and being admitted on Saturday. A person like me would typically stay for a week. However, God only required me to sit for a few days for me to realize that this was my last wake-up call.

There, I could not hide. To avoid being held any longer, I had to abide by all the rules. I was afraid. However, I prayed to God for understanding for the first time. His power. "Lord, align my will with Yours," I prayed. I meant it, too. I had previously prayed, but not in this way. Not from a position of capitulation.

God made it clear to me there that I was not destined to practice law. I had that dream, but it was not his dream. He guided me toward my actual purpose by using the breakdown.

Oddly enough, my advisor advised me to thoroughly study God's word back in January. In April, I had to learn the hard way.

My dad yelled when he learned. I sobbed. He thought I "had it all," so he did not understand why I would do something like that. However, I did not know what to do.

What was broken was not fixed by the college. And my advisor was the only person I could speak with. He was there, but I didn't want to be a burden.

"For a person who attend church every Sunday can't be struggling I'm the one struggling," my mother said. However, I was. The wrong church was where I was.

Furthermore, I was not necessarily okay just because I smiled online. As a first-generation college student, no one understood the pressure I was under.

I realized then neither of my parents would see me at home. I was returning to God.

I hoped that my advisor would learn about it and even come to assist me. My idea was more so come break me out of this clinic.

However, God had other ideas.

I went straight to his office and told him everything after I eventually got out. He was the way the Holy Spirit returned me to the Father at that moment.

God had been waiting for that very moment.

This time, I was baptized for real. In his name. And even though the enemy returned with vengeance, I had something more profound this time. a genuine relationship. A true comprehension.

I am writing this now for that reason.

Chapter

10

THE REALIZATION OF TRUTH

I was discovering who I was, but I was also discovering who God was. My story fragments were now a part of a larger awakening rather than isolated episodes of suffering. I had to die to the life I had created without God and be born again into the one He was offering me, which was one of the most profound realizations I had ever experienced.

Baptism came to symbolize that. Not only ceremony, not just water—but symbolism. That was when I said, "I am not who I used to be." My death to sin and resurrection to a new life in Christ were represented by my baptism. Being lowered into the water symbolized the burial of my former self, much like Christ was buried and rose again. My new identity, one that was molded by grace rather than shame, abandonment, or people-pleasing, was reflected in my rising up.

I had believed that I had to earn my recovery. However, I came to understand that salvation is not based on deeds, customs, or even being "good enough." It is obtained only by faith in Jesus. I wasn't saved by baptism. It was what demonstrated to the world that I had already been saved, pardoned, and set free. It was an outward manifestation of an internal transformation that had begun to occur within my spirit. It had to be done the proper way.

And the proper way to become a true child of God is to be baptized in a church that carries God's name, God's Word, and God's presence. And if I had not begun studying His Word for myself or sensed the strong convictions He put in my heart, I would not have known that.

See, baptism was taking place in various forms even before the Christian church was founded. It is likely that you have heard about Jesus' baptism in the Jordan River. Jews practiced symbolic cleansings and ritual baths. However, everything changed when Jesus rose from the dead. The resurrection marked the start of a new command, not just a passing moment.

That is what initially confused me.

I recall asking myself, "Why am I feeling so pressured to get baptized in a church when Jesus was baptized in a river?" However, God then revealed to me: Because it became a command following His resurrection. It was now a component of a commission rather than merely symbolic. A necessity.

I had completely missed that part, and to be honest, so did a lot of people.

"Go therefore and make disciples of all nations, baptizing them in the name of the Father, and of the Son, and of the Holy Spirit," was God's explicit directive to His followers. Matthew 28:19

Then the church came into being. Furthermore, baptism evolved from being merely water to becoming a means of entering Christ's body. a spiritual awakening that is in accordance with God's Word and encircled by a truth-based community.

Acts 2; Ephesians 4:4–6; Romans 6.

They all make it clear.

"Just as you were called to one hope when you were called— one Lord, one faith, one baptism—there is one body and one Spirit." (Ephesians 4:4–6) (NIV).

That "one body" is the church, which is a group of believers bound together by the same truth rather than a structure or a denomination. The same Spirit. The same Christ. Rather than using titles, labels, or divergent ideologies, that verse calls us to acknowledge our common identity and dedication to Christ via His church.

Then we have Acts 2:46:

"And they received their food with joyful and giving hearts day by day, going to the temple together and breaking bread in their homes." (NIV)

That verse really got to me.

Daily. Not every week. Not once every month. They carved out time each day for spiritual interaction. That made me realize that spirituality is not just for Sundays. Everyday counts. Walking with God every day includes even five minutes of prayer, a moment of introspection, or reading a verse.

"*Going to the temple together*" equates to regular collective worship.

"Breaking bread in their homes" refers to camaraderie and unity.

I was messed up by that last one. Why do we only partake in the Lord's Supper once a month, or less, if the early Christians did so every day? Communion is more than just a custom. It is revered. It is honoring Him. What if Jesus returned and asked, "When was the last time you truly remembered Me?" Was the question raised for me?

I was at fault. guilty of merely following the procedures. of failing to appreciate the significance of what He outlined in detail.

In addition, I had to unlearn something that many people would rather not discuss.

Churches are classified as either denominational or non-denominational.

Do you know what I found? The Bible does not contain either of those. Those words? Those divisions? We made them. However, God stated unequivocally: One body. One Spirit. Just one Lord. One religion. One baptism.

There is not much more straightforward than that.

I have no judgment to offer. I am not here to disparage someone's background or beliefs.

Before you speak, take the time to find out the truth.

I am overseeing leading a better life now that I know better. And impart what I have discovered.

I understand if you do not accept it. I had to say it, though. Because you cannot return to your previous way of life once the truth is met. I cannot deny what God has shown me. I cannot keep quiet about what nearly destroyed my soul.

This phase of my life is about knowing, not speculating, or repeating what I have been told. Being aware of what God wants. Being able to walk in His presence. And understanding what obedience is.

Chapter

11

THE CHILD HE CALLED BACK

This story was both my building and my breaking.

My fall and my journey of faith.

That was when I discovered that God occasionally permits failure because He is aware that the breakthrough lies beyond.

Yes, I still have difficulties.

Yes, there are still times when I experience spiritual warfare, melancholy, and silence.

I walk differently now, though. I walk with others.

Thanks to God, I am succeeding.

I used to believe that being a follower of Christ only involved believing.

However, I discovered that faith without action is meaningless.

Before I allowed God to unteach me what the world had taught me, I was unaware of the truth.

Until I opened His Word, confronted my convictions, and did what He said, not just what other people thought I should do.

Everything changed at that point.

I used to think that simply believing was enough to be a follower of Christ.

However, belief is meaningless without action.

Before I let God rewire everything I had learned—until I studied His Word, confronted my beliefs, and obeyed what He honestly said, not just what I was told by others—I did not fully comprehend the truth.

God invited me into His light rather than merely dragging me out of the shadows.

Something changed deep within me when I was baptized in His name, in His body, the church.

It was a true surrender.

It had to do with relationships. Actually. rooted. Redeeming.

Tradition or denomination had nothing to do with this.

Truth is at issue here.

One body. One Spirit. Just one Lord. One religion. One baptism.

And accountability accompanied that reality.

My Godmother had been praying for this begging God to help me grow into the leader He intended me to be.

To support me in living for Him. To assist me in transforming the world.

For a long time, it meant addressing broken laws, fighting policies, and changing systems.

I now realize, however, that God was calling me to something more profound.

To guide His followers back to reality.

To connect with people who, like me, believed they were walking in His footsteps but were going in the wrong direction.

And a person who has experienced it firsthand is the best person to assist them.

Someone who made a mistake before she made a correct one.

Someone who discovered that true freedom lies in surrender rather than routine.

I am so grateful that I understood at last.

And I have not finished yet.

I am walking with a purpose now.

Living rooted in harmony.

I still cry sometimes, but I know who I can cry with.

Even though I rely on God's strength rather than my own, there are still times when I feel weak.

Clarity is the difference now. conviction. And a serenity that is based on presence—God's presence—rather than perfection.

I am still standing because of it.

That is the reason I continue to write.

Because there is someone else out there now, confused, exhausted, surviving rather than living.

Find out what God truly desires from you.

He is waiting, not angry.

To put you in a position, do not punish you.

To call you, not to crush you.

And he could call you too if he called me back.

I am responding this time as the child He called back because this is The Final Awakening I Couldn't Ignore.

She is up.

Dear God,

I am grateful that even when I gave up on myself, you never gave up on me. If I had a thousand tongues, it still wouldn't be enough to thank you.

You were there through all the dark times, all the silent cries, all the hidden wounds. You loved me when I didn't feel deserving of love, held me when I felt abandoned, and saw me when I was forgotten. When I strayed too far, you called me back, and when I didn't answer, you patiently waited.

This book is your story, not just mine. It's the tale of how You helped me get over my suffering, break my silence, and find meaning in areas I believed were irreparably damaged.

I appreciate you taking advantage of my brokenness to promote healing. Thank You for demonstrating to me that who I am in You, not what happened to me, is who I am.

I remembered; you reminded me. I've been picked. Someone called me.

This realization... I was unable to ignore it.

From the bottom of my heart,

Da'Ziyah

IN LOVING MEMORY OF
MAMA J

Dear Godmother,

Since 2017, I've clung to your final words to me: "We're going to start our girls night." You informed me that although you hadn't been there as much as you planned, you would begin. I thought we would have that time. You suddenly became ill, though, and left us before we had a chance.

You asked God to grant me leadership. To adhere to Christ. To alter the course of events. 20 years ago up until you passed you never stopped praying and believing. Here I am now, living out the very prayers you said over my head. But knowing that you're not present to witness it hurts.

I cherish you. I cannot express how much I miss you. And I sincerely hope that you will be pleased with the woman I'm growing into.

Love always,

Your Goddaughter

IN LOVING MEMORY OF MY GRANDAD.
James Terry

Dear Grandad,

I wish you were still with us. I know you would be so proud of me. Anything I asked I'm sure it would have been a "yeah, yeah, yeah Green just go get it out the bank". You were my first father; you showed me what it meant to be well-cared for, and cherished. You always made sure I had everything I needed or desired. You made sure I was always taken care of, no matter how big or small my dreams were.

You and Aunt Dot were able to create a mystical atmosphere during Christmas. She always made sure I had a brand-new Easy-Bake Oven every year, and I eagerly anticipated it. Like the new bike I could always rely on, even if I outgrew it too quickly or someone ran it over before December arrived, it was tradition.

I still carry those moments with me. They were indications that I was seen, loved, and thought of, and they went beyond simple presents.

I really do miss you, Granddaddy.

Always with love,
Da'Ziyah

To All of My middle school/high school teachers Who Had Faith in Me—

Thank you.

You saw me when I was a young girl, walking into school with more than just a backpack. You paid attention. You didn't have to take me under your wing, but you did. More than you could have imagined, every encouraging word, every hallway check-in, and every instance in which you made me feel important got me through.

The battles became heavier as I grew older. You continued to support me when my life changed, and I was on the verge of being sent away. You persisted in trying to reach me.

To all the encouraging seeds you have ever sown in me. To faith. To have a purpose.

Without the village of teachers who saw more in me than what my circumstances attempted to portray, I would not have been able to succeed. I appreciate you helping to keep me going.

From the bottom of my heart,
Da'Ziyah Johnson
Everett. Mixon.
Shakespeare. Coakley.

Dear Mcdaniels,

I'm grateful that you took me into your arms during my freshman year, not as your advisee but as your child as well even though you have children of your own. You accepted me long before I realized who I was going to be. You invested the time to get to know me as a person as well as a student. Even when I lacked the strength to present myself as my best self, you never abandoned me.

You never stopped telling me that I was loved, not just by you but also by other people, and you saw something in me that I couldn't yet see in myself. Your concern for your students extends well beyond the classroom. It's genuine and uncommon.

I genuinely don't know what I would have done in your absence. In times when I was walking in darkness, you were a beacon of light. I appreciate your love, support, and belief in me during this entire process.

THE AWAKENING I COULDN'T IGNORE

Dear my Cobie Co,

For as long as I can remember, I have loved you. You were more than just my cousin; you were like my brother from the time we were young. I wouldn't trade those memories for anything because we did everything together. Making sure you were safe and having fun meant the world to me, so I was always right there with you, running around outside like one of the boys, even though I was only a girl.

However, you had no idea when you were in that car accident. It completely rocked me. I've never cried out to God so loudly as I did when I saw you in that state. I pleaded with Him to keep you alive. He gave you another chance, as I begged him to do.

However, I continued to stray from Him even after that miracle. I should have been awakened by that moment, but I chose to ignore it. Nevertheless, God's mercy was revealed. I sincerely don't know what I'd do without you, so I thank God every day that you're still with me.

Cobie, you've always held a particular place in my heart. Not only because of who you are, but also because of everything we've experienced together, you will always be my favorite. #cobiestrong

With all of my affection,
Da'Ziyah.

Dear God, A Prayer for the One Who Is Still Fighting

I appreciate that even when I was slipping, you never let go of me. I'm grateful for every door that has been closed to keep me safe and every one that has been opened to bring me nearer to You.

Now I raise the one reading this. The person who is numb, angry, exhausted, or lost. The one with hidden tears and silent battles. Give them peace. Prove to them that You are close, even now, especially now.

When they feel weak, give them strength. Clarity in areas of ambiguity. Where there is hurt, there is healing. Raise your voice above the lies. Tell them they were chosen, loved, and made with a purpose. God, I ask you to turn every person that is reading this into the person you created them to be and not the person they want to be.

Remind them that this is only the page turning and that their story is not over.

In Jesus Name,
Amen

Wait, before you close this book…

I want to make it very clear that I am not God.

I'm not your preacher. I'm a girl who has experienced some things and survived them. This book is not a substitute for the truth; it is my testimony.

Don't stop here, then. Get your Bible open.

Say a prayer. Pose inquiries. If you have to, cry. Look for answers.

And above all, attend church, a real church that represents Christ. Seek out a genuine community that reminds you that you are not alone and teaches the Word.

I pray that this story will encourage you to pursue your own ultimate awakening, one that comes straight from God, even though what helped me might not look the same to you.

Because he is still writing your story, I assure you.

With affection,
Da'Ziyah

www.ingramcontent.com/pod-product-compliance
Lightning Source LLC
Chambersburg PA
CBHW031357160426
42813CB00081B/9